Christian Book Series Self Help Bible Study Guide on Heaven

KJV Bible Based Verses & Lessons for Men, Women, Couples, Teens, Kids, & Beginners

by Brian Mahoney

TABLE OF CONTENTS

Page

INTRODUCTION.. 11

Part 1 OT Scriptures on Heaven...................... 20

Part 2 OT Scriptures on Heaven...................... 30

Part 3 NT Scriptures on Heaven...................... 40

Part 4 NT Scriptures on Heaven...................... 67

Part 5 NT Scriptures on Heaven...................... 88

Part 6 Bible Life Lesson on Heaven................. 106

Part 7 Top 10 Bible Verses on Heaven............ 115

Part 8 Bible Quiz on Heaven........................... 123

CONCLUSION.. 130

About the Author

Brian Mahoney has spent a quarter century preaching and teaching the word of God in non denominational Churches of Christ through out the United States.

He served two overseas tours in the United States Army, then worked for the Government for almost two decades and has a IT degree in Computer Programming and is completing another degree in Business.

He has 2 sons. Both his sons accepted the gospel of Jesus Christ and were baptized as teenagers. Attending the University of Virginia, Columbia Law School and Radford University. Between them they have gone on to get degrees in Law, Physical Therapy and Engineering.

Disclaimer Notice

This book was written as a guide and for information, educational and entertainment purposes only. No warranties of any kind are expressed or implied.

Readers acknowledge that the author is not engaging in the rendering of legal, financial, medical or professional advice, and the information in this book is not meant to take the place of any professional advice. If advice is needed in any of these fields, you are advised to seek the services of a professional.

While the author has attempted to make the information in this book as accurate as possible, no guarantee is given as to the accuracy or currency of any individual item. Laws and procedures related to business, health and well being are constantly changing.

Therefore, in no event shall the author of this book be liable for any special, indirect, or consequential damages or any damages whatsoever in connection with the use of the information herein provided.

All Rights Reserved

No part of this book may be used or reproduced in any manner whatsoever without the written permission of the author.

Copyright © 2022 Brian Mahoney
All rights reserved.

DEDICATION

This book is dedicated to my Father

Ulester Love Mahoney Sr.

He instilled a love for God, and taught

as much by his actions as he did with his words.

ACKNOWLEDGMENTS

I WOULD LIKE TO ACKNOWLEDGE ALL THE HARD WORK OF THE MEN AND WOMEN OF THE UNITED STATES MILITARY, WHO RISK THEIR LIVES ON A DAILY BASIS, TO MAKE THE WORLD A SAFER PLACE.

INTRODUCTION

INTRODUCTION

I want to thank you for purchasing

Christian Book Series Self Help Bible Study Guide on **Heaven**, KJV Bible Based Verses & Lessons for Men, Women, Couples, Teens, Kids, & Beginners

This is just one of a series of books I have created to give bible answers to bible topics or questions.

With this book you will Discover...

* The best Old Testament Bible Verses on **Heaven**!
* The best New Testament Bible Verses on **Heaven**!
* We reveal the top 10 Scriptures on **Heaven** voted online from Christians around the world!
* A Bible chapter, set of scriptures or story to best illustrate **Heaven** principles in action!
* A easy quiz to aid in retention of all the knowledge you discover.
* One final recap to further help elevate your understanding of what the Bible says about this amazing Topic!

Just a few of the many uses...

INTRODUCTION

* A perfect gift for family and friends
* Deepen your personal Bible Study
* A teaching aid for Bible Study Classes
* A teaching aid for counseling
* Use for morning meditation
* Use the AUDIO BOOK version for sleep affirmation

This book will help beginners to get off of milk and begin to eat meat!

Hebrews 5:12

"For when for the time ye ought to be teachers, ye have need that one teach you again which be the first principles of the oracles of God; and are become such as have need of milk, and not of strong meat."

1 Peter 3:15

" But sanctify the Lord God in your hearts: and be ready always to give an answer to every man that asketh you a reason of the hope that is in you with meekness and fear:"

INTRODUCTION

Now is the time to grow spiritually! Discover more of what the Bible says about **Heaven** so you can be ready share the Good News when the opportunity arises!

Throughout this book at the end of several sections will be a Bonus Bible Basics Lesson!

The first of these will be Bonus Bible Basics Lesson: The Bible The Church & Christians!

The bible is a book of books, consisting of the Old and New Testaments.

The Bible takes its name from the Latin Biblia ('book' or 'books') which comes from the Greek Ta Biblia ('the books') traced to the Phoenician port city of Gebal, known as Byblos to the Greeks. Writing became associated with Byblos as an exporter of papyrus (used in writing) and the Greek name for papyrus was bublos.

Now if you ever get the chance to visit Epcot Center at Walt Disney World Florida, the Phoenician section of the Space Earth ride will take on a whole new meaning!

INTRODUCTION

The bible is divided into sections and they are:

The Old Testament
It's Sections:
The Law: Genesis - Deuteronomy
History: Joshua - Esther
Poetry: Job - Ecclesiates
Major prophets: Isaiah - Daniel
Minor prophets: Hosea - Malachi

The New Testament
It's Sections:
The Gospels: Matthew - John
History: Acts
The Epistles: Romans - Jude
Prophecy: Revelation

What is the Church?

(eck la see a) the church the called out
Ekklesia is a Greek word defined as "a called-out assembly or congregation." Ekklesia is commonly translated as "church" in the New Testament. For example, Acts 11:26 says that "Barnabas and Saul met with the church [ekklesia]" in Antioch.

INTRODUCTION

Why are we called Christians?

Acts 11:26

And when he had found him, he brought him unto Antioch. And it came to pass, that a whole year they assembled themselves with the church, and taught much people. And the disciples were called **Christians** first in Antioch.

Why do we assemble for worship service?

Hebrews 10:25-26

25 Not forsaking the assembling of ourselves together, as the manner of some is; but exhorting one another: and so much the more, as ye see the day approaching.

26 For if we sin wilfully after that we have received the knowledge of the truth, there remaineth no more sacrifice for sins,

INTRODUCTION

Why do we worship on Sunday?

1 Corinthians 16:2

2 Upon the first day of the week let every one of you lay by him in store, as God hath prospered him, that there be no gatherings when I come.

Acts 20:6-7

6 And we sailed away from Philippi after the days of unleavened bread, and came unto them to Troas in five days; where we abode seven days.

7 And upon the first day of the week, when the disciples came together to break bread, Paul preached unto them, ready to depart on the morrow; and continued his speech until midnight.

So they were there seven days, and they did something on the first day they did not do on the others, and that is they came together to break bread and Paul preached to them.

INTRODUCTION

Why should we continue to read and study the Bible? Because....

"16 All scripture is given by inspiration of God, and is profitable for doctrine, for reproof, for correction, for instruction in righteousness:

17 That the man of God may be perfect, thoroughly furnished unto all good works."

2 Timothy 3:16-17

This concludes the Introduction... Now let's get started with Part 1 of Bible Verses about **Heaven**.

PART 1
OLD TESTAMENT
BIBLE VERSES:
CREATION AND
DWELLING

OT BIBLE VERSES: CREATION & DWELLING

GOD'S CREATION

Genesis 1:1

In the beginning God created the heaven and the earth.

Isaiah 65:17

17 For, behold, I create new heavens and a new earth: and the former shall not be remembered, nor come into mind.

Isaiah 45:18

18 For thus saith the Lord that created the heavens; God himself that formed the earth and made it; he hath established it, he created it not in vain, he formed it to be inhabited: I am the Lord; and there is none else.

Jeremiah 10:12

12 He hath made the earth by his power, he hath established the world by his wisdom, and hath stretched out the heavens by his discretion.

OT BIBLE VERSES: CREATION & DWELLING

Nehemiah 9:6

6 Thou, even thou, art Lord alone; thou hast made heaven, the heaven of heavens, with all their host, the earth, and all things that are therein, the seas, and all that is therein, and thou preservest them all; and the host of heaven worshippeth thee.

GOD'S DWELLING PLACE

1 Kings 8:30

30 And hearken thou to the supplication of thy servant, and of thy people Israel, when they shall pray toward this place: and hear thou in heaven thy dwelling place: and when thou hearest, forgive.

2 Chronicles 6:30

30 Then hear thou from heaven thy dwelling place, and forgive, and render unto every man according unto all his ways, whose heart thou knowest; (for thou only knowest the hearts of the children of men:)

OT BIBLE VERSES: CREATION & DWELLING

Lamentations 3:41

41 Let us lift up our heart with our hands unto God in the heavens.

This completes part 1 **Heaven Old Testament Bible Verses King James Version**

BIBLE BONUS LESSON: Rightly Dividing the Truth

BIBLE BONUS LESSON

Welcome to the first of several short Bonus Bible Lessons by Wesley Helfenbein. These lessons will appear at the end of many parts of this book to help you to better learn and understand the bible. Now let's get started!

Rightly Dividing the Truth

Matthew 7:21-27

21 Not every one that saith unto me, Lord, Lord, shall enter into the kingdom of heaven; but he that doeth the will of my Father which is in heaven.

22 Many will say to me in that day, Lord, Lord, have we not prophesied in thy name? and in thy name have cast out devils? and in thy name done many wonderful works?

23 And then will I profess unto them, I never knew you: depart from me, ye that work iniquity.

24 Therefore whosoever heareth these sayings of mine, and doeth them, I will liken him unto a wise man, which built his house upon a rock:

25 And the rain descended, and the floods came, and the winds blew, and beat upon that house; and it fell not: for it was founded upon a rock.

26 And every one that heareth these sayings of mine, and doeth them not, shall be likened unto a foolish man, which built his house upon the sand:

BIBLE BONUS LESSON

27 And the rain descended, and the floods came, and the winds blew, and beat upon that house; and it fell: and great was the fall of it.

2 Timothy 2:15

Study to shew thyself approved unto God, a workman that needeth not to be ashamed, rightly dividing the word of truth.

We must rightly divide the truth. Matthew 7:21-27 shows us the danger of wrongly dividing the truth. How sad to see a person who believes that Jesus is Lord and is doing what he believes is many wonderful works in the name of the Lord, only to hear, in the day of judgement "depart from me".

2 Timothy 2:15 tells us that the solution to understanding bible truth is not just to read the Bible but to study it. Here are some strategies on how to improve our understanding of the bible, and rightly divide the truth.

I.   Read the Bible frequently.

II. Two or Three Witnesses

III. Read the Entire Bible.

IV. Do not add to or take away.

V.   Faith with out works is dead.

BIBLE BONUS LESSON

I. Read the Bible frequently.

Acts 17:11

These were more noble than those in Thessalonica, in that they received the word with all readiness of mind, and searched the scriptures daily, whether those things were so.

Joshua 1:7-8

7 Only be thou strong and very courageous, that thou mayest observe to do according to all the law, which Moses my servant commanded thee: turn not from it to the right hand or to the left, that thou mayest prosper withersoever thou goest

8 This book of the law shall not depart out of thy mouth; but thou shalt meditate therein day and night, that thou mayest observe to do according to all that is written therein: for then thou shalt make thy way prosperous, and then thou shalt have good success.

Later on in the book of Joshua we learn that someone did turn either right or left from the word. Not only did it cost that person and their family their life, the entire congregation suffered.

Notice that the scriptures use the words "daily" and "day and night" to emphasize the frequency needed to understanding.

BIBLE BONUS LESSON

It is nice to attend bible classes and hear sermons, but you have to search the scriptures for yourself to help in maximizing your understanding.

Psalm 119:10-12

10 With my whole heart have I sought thee: O let me not wander from thy commandments.

11 Thy word have I hid in mine heart, that I might not sin against thee.

12 Blessed art thou, O Lord: teach me thy statutes.

PART 2
OLD TESTAMENT BIBLE VERSES: SALVATION & PSALMS

OT BIBLE VERSES: SALVATION & PSALMS

OUR SALVATION & PSALMS

2 Kings 2:11

11 And it came to pass, as they still went on, and talked, that, behold, there appeared a chariot of fire, and horses of fire, and parted them both asunder; and Elijah went up by a whirlwind into heaven.

Isaiah 25:6-9

6 And in this mountain shall the Lord of hosts make unto all people a feast of fat things, a feast of wines on the lees, of fat things full of marrow, of wines on the lees well refined.

7 And he will destroy in this mountain the face of the covering cast over all people, and the vail that is spread over all nations.

8 He will swallow up death in victory; and the Lord God will wipe away tears from off all faces; and the rebuke of his people shall he take away from off all the earth: for the Lord hath spoken it.

OT BIBLE VERSES: SALVATION & PSALMS

9 And it shall be said in that day, Lo, this is our God; we have waited for him, and he will save us: this is the Lord; we have waited for him, we will be glad and rejoice in his salvation.

2 Samuel 12:18-23

18 And it came to pass on the seventh day, that the child died. And the servants of David feared to tell him that the child was dead: for they said, Behold, while the child was yet alive, we spake unto him, and he would not hearken unto our voice: how will he then vex himself, if we tell him that the child is dead?

19 But when David saw that his servants whispered, David perceived that the child was dead: therefore David said unto his servants, Is the child dead? And they said, He is dead.

20 Then David arose from the earth, and washed, and anointed himself, and changed his apparel, and came into the house of the Lord, and worshipped: then he came to his own house; and when he required, they set bread before him, and he did eat.

OT BIBLE VERSES: SALVATION & PSALMS

21 Then said his servants unto him, What thing is this that thou hast done? thou didst fast and weep for the child, while it was alive; but when the child was dead, thou didst rise and eat bread.

22 And he said, While the child was yet alive, I fasted and wept: for I said, Who can tell whether God will be gracious to me, that the child may live?

23 But now he is dead, wherefore should I fast? can I bring him back again? I shall go to him, but he shall not return to me.

HEAVEN - PSALMS

Psalm 16:11

11 Thou wilt shew me the path of life: in thy presence is fulness of joy; at thy right hand there are pleasures for evermore.

OT BIBLE VERSES: SALVATION & PSALMS

Psalm 33:6

6 By the word of the Lord were the heavens made; and all the host of them by the breath of his mouth.

Psalm 19:1

The heavens declare the glory of God; and the firmament sheweth his handywork.

Psalm 103:11

11 For as the heaven is high above the earth, so great is his mercy toward them that fear him.

Psalm 73:24

24 Thou shalt guide me with thy counsel, and afterward receive me to glory.

Psalm 20:6

6 Now know I that the Lord saveth his anointed; he will hear him from his holy heaven with the saving strength of his right hand.

OT BIBLE VERSES: SALVATION & PSALMS

Psalm 8:3

3 When I consider thy heavens, the work of thy fingers, the moon and the stars, which thou hast ordained;

this completes part 2 Heaven Old Testament Bible Verses King James Version

BIBLE BONUS LESSON: Two or Three Witnesses

BIBLE BONUS LESSON

II. Two or Three Witnesses

Deuteronomy 17:6

At the mouth of two witnesses, or three witnesses, shall he that is worthy of death be put to death; but at the mouth of one witness he shall not be put to death.

Matthew 18:16

But if he will not hear thee, then take with thee one or two more, that in the mouth of two or three witnesses every word may be established.

Malachi 3:6

For I am the Lord, I change not; therefore ye sons of Jacob are not consumed.

Hebrews 13:8

Jesus Christ the same yesterday, and to day, and for ever.

The word of God is consistent. When it is the truth, it is not hard to find multiple scriptures to support it.

When it is the truth, it is not hard to show a consistent line of reasoning from the Old Testament to the New Testament.

That is why through out this book you will see multiple scriptures used on every topic covered.

BIBLE BONUS LESSON

God does not change. Some of His instruction does. The instruction you give toddler is different from the instruction you give a 10 year old. The instruction you give a 10 year old is different from the instruction you give a teenager. The instruction you give a teenager is different from the instruction you give a 25 year old young adult. You did not change. The child did.

As a person gets older you expect them to mature and be able to handle more responsibility, building on the teaching from their youth.

"The Old Testament is the New Testament concealed. The New Testament is the Old Testament revealed."

Gospel Preacher the Late Johnny Ramsey...

PART 3
NEW TESTAMENT BIBLE VERSES: THE GOSPELS

NT BIBLE VERSES: THE GOSPELS

The book of Matthew

Matthew 19:14

14 But Jesus said, Suffer little children, and forbid them not, to come unto me: for of such is the kingdom of heaven.

Matthew 6:9

9 After this manner therefore pray ye: Our Father which art in heaven, Hallowed be thy name.

Matthew 5:8

8 Blessed are the pure in heart: for they shall see God.

Matthew 3:12

12 Whose fan is in his hand, and he will throughly purge his floor, and gather his wheat into the garner; but he will burn up the chaff with unquenchable fire.

NT BIBLE VERSES: THE GOSPELS

Matthew 11:25

25 At that time Jesus answered and said, I thank thee, O Father, Lord of heaven and earth, because thou hast hid these things from the wise and prudent, and hast revealed them unto babes.

Matthew 25:46

46 And these shall go away into everlasting punishment: but the righteous into life eternal.

Matthew 18:10

10 Take heed that ye despise not one of these little ones; for I say unto you, That in heaven their angels do always behold the face of my Father which is in heaven.

Matthew 13:43

43 Then shall the righteous shine forth as the sun in the kingdom of their Father. Who hath ears to hear, let him hear.

NT BIBLE VERSES: THE GOSPELS

Matthew 19:21

21 Jesus said unto him, If thou wilt be perfect, go and sell that thou hast, and give to the poor, and thou shalt have treasure in heaven: and come and follow me.

Matthew 6:19-21

19 Lay not up for yourselves treasures upon earth, where moth and rust doth corrupt, and where thieves break through and steal:

20 But lay up for yourselves treasures in heaven, where neither moth nor rust doth corrupt, and where thieves do not break through nor steal:

21 For where your treasure is, there will your heart be also.

Matthew 25:31-46

31 When the Son of man shall come in his glory, and all the holy angels with him, then shall he sit upon the throne of his glory:

NT BIBLE VERSES: THE GOSPELS

32 And before him shall be gathered all nations: and he shall separate them one from another, as a shepherd divideth his sheep from the goats:

33 And he shall set the sheep on his right hand, but the goats on the left.

34 Then shall the King say unto them on his right hand, Come, ye blessed of my Father, inherit the kingdom prepared for you from the foundation of the world:

35 For I was an hungred, and ye gave me meat: I was thirsty, and ye gave me drink: I was a stranger, and ye took me in:

36 Naked, and ye clothed me: I was sick, and ye visited me: I was in prison, and ye came unto me.

37 Then shall the righteous answer him, saying, Lord, when saw we thee an hungred, and fed thee? or thirsty, and gave thee drink?

38 When saw we thee a stranger, and took thee in? or naked, and clothed thee?

NT BIBLE VERSES: THE GOSPELS

39 Or when saw we thee sick, or in prison, and came unto thee?

40 And the King shall answer and say unto them, Verily I say unto you, Inasmuch as ye have done it unto one of the least of these my brethren, ye have done it unto me.

41 Then shall he say also unto them on the left hand, Depart from me, ye cursed, into everlasting fire, prepared for the devil and his angels:

42 For I was an hungred, and ye gave me no meat: I was thirsty, and ye gave me no drink:

43 I was a stranger, and ye took me not in: naked, and ye clothed me not: sick, and in prison, and ye visited me not.

44 Then shall they also answer him, saying, Lord, when saw we thee an hungred, or athirst, or a stranger, or naked, or sick, or in prison, and did not minister unto thee?

45 Then shall he answer them, saying, Verily I say unto you, Inasmuch as ye did it not to one of the least of these, ye did it not to me.

NT BIBLE VERSES: THE GOSPELS

46 And these shall go away into everlasting punishment: but the righteous into life eternal.

The book of Luke

Luke 10:20

20 Notwithstanding in this rejoice not, that the spirits are subject unto you; but rather rejoice, because your names are written in heaven.

6. Luke 23:43

43 And Jesus said unto him, Verily I say unto thee, Today shalt thou be with me in paradise.

Luke 12:32-34

32 Fear not, little flock; for it is your Father's good pleasure to give you the kingdom.

33 Sell that ye have, and give alms; provide yourselves bags which wax not old, a treasure in the heavens that faileth not, where no thief approacheth, neither moth corrupteth.

NT BIBLE VERSES: THE GOSPELS

34 For where your treasure is, there will your heart be also.

Luke 16:19-30

19 There was a certain rich man, which was clothed in purple and fine linen, and fared sumptuously every day:

20 And there was a certain beggar named Lazarus, which was laid at his gate, full of sores,

21 And desiring to be fed with the crumbs which fell from the rich man's table: moreover the dogs came and licked his sores.

22 And it came to pass, that the beggar died, and was carried by the angels into Abraham's bosom: the rich man also died, and was buried;

23 And in hell he lift up his eyes, being in torments, and seeth Abraham afar off, and Lazarus in his bosom.

NT BIBLE VERSES: THE GOSPELS

24 And he cried and said, Father Abraham, have mercy on me, and send Lazarus, that he may dip the tip of his finger in water, and cool my tongue; for I am tormented in this flame.

25 But Abraham said, Son, remember that thou in thy lifetime receivedst thy good things, and likewise Lazarus evil things: but now he is comforted, and thou art tormented.

26 And beside all this, between us and you there is a great gulf fixed: so that they which would pass from hence to you cannot; neither can they pass to us, that would come from thence.

27 Then he said, I pray thee therefore, father, that thou wouldest send him to my father's house:

28 For I have five brethren; that he may testify unto them, lest they also come into this place of torment.

29 Abraham saith unto him, They have Moses and the prophets; let them hear them.

NT BIBLE VERSES: THE GOSPELS

30 And he said, Nay, father Abraham: but if one went unto them from the dead, they will repent.

The book of John

John 14:2

2 In my Father's house are many mansions: if it were not so, I would have told you. I go to prepare a place for you.

4. John 3:16

16 For God so loved the world, that he gave his only begotten Son, that whosoever believeth in him should not perish, but have everlasting life.

John 3:13

13 And no man hath ascended up to heaven, but he that came down from heaven, even the Son of man which is in heaven.

NT BIBLE VERSES: THE GOSPELS

John 3:36

36 He that believeth on the Son hath everlasting life: and he that believeth not the Son shall not see life; but the wrath of God abideth on him.

John 10:28

28 And I give unto them eternal life; and they shall never perish, neither shall any man pluck them out of my hand.

John 13:36

36 Simon Peter said unto him, Lord, whither goest thou? Jesus answered him, Whither I go, thou canst not follow me now; but thou shalt follow me afterwards.

John 14:1-4

Let not your heart be troubled: ye believe in God, believe also in me.

2 In my Father's house are many mansions: if it were not so, I would have told you. I go to prepare a place for you.

NT BIBLE VERSES: THE GOSPELS

3 And if I go and prepare a place for you, I will come again, and receive you unto myself; that where I am, there ye may be also.

4 And whither I go ye know, and the way ye know.

John 6:47-50

47 Verily, verily, I say unto you, He that believeth on me hath everlasting life.

48 I am that bread of life.

49 Your fathers did eat manna in the wilderness, and are dead.

50 This is the bread which cometh down from heaven, that a man may eat thereof, and not die.

John 6:50-71

50 This is the bread which cometh down from heaven, that a man may eat thereof, and not die.

NT BIBLE VERSES: THE GOSPELS

51 I am the living bread which came down from heaven: if any man eat of this bread, he shall live for ever: and the bread that I will give is my flesh, which I will give for the life of the world.

52 The Jews therefore strove among themselves, saying, How can this man give us his flesh to eat?

53 Then Jesus said unto them, Verily, verily, I say unto you, Except ye eat the flesh of the Son of man, and drink his blood, ye have no life in you.

54 Whoso eateth my flesh, and drinketh my blood, hath eternal life; and I will raise him up at the last day.

55 For my flesh is meat indeed, and my blood is drink indeed.

56 He that eateth my flesh, and drinketh my blood, dwelleth in me, and I in him.

57 As the living Father hath sent me, and I live by the Father: so he that eateth me, even he shall live by me.

NT BIBLE VERSES: THE GOSPELS

58 This is that bread which came down from heaven: not as your fathers did eat manna, and are dead: he that eateth of this bread shall live for ever.

59 These things said he in the synagogue, as he taught in Capernaum.

60 Many therefore of his disciples, when they had heard this, said, This is an hard saying; who car hear it?

61 When Jesus knew in himself that his disciples murmured at it, he said unto them, Doth this offend you?

62 What and if ye shall see the Son of man ascend up where he was before?

63 It is the spirit that quickeneth; the flesh profiteth nothing: the words that I speak unto you, they are spirit, and they are life.

64 But there are some of you that believe not. For Jesus knew from the beginning who they were that believed not, and who should betray him.

NT BIBLE VERSES: THE GOSPELS

65 And he said, Therefore said I unto you, that no man can come unto me, except it were given unto him of my Father.

66 From that time many of his disciples went back, and walked no more with him.

67 Then said Jesus unto the twelve, Will ye also go away?

68 Then Simon Peter answered him, Lord, to whom shall we go? thou hast the words of eternal life.

69 And we believe and are sure that thou art that Christ, the Son of the living God.

70 Jesus answered them, Have not I chosen you twelve, and one of you is a devil?

71 He spake of Judas Iscariot the son of Simon: for he it was that should betray him, being one of the twelve.

BIBLE BONUS LESSON:

Read The Entire Bible

BIBLE BONUS LESSON

III. Read the Entire Bible

John 3:16

For God so loved the world, that he gave his only begotten Son, that whosoever believeth in him should not perish, but have everlasting life.

After reading John 3:16 it would be easy for me to conclude that all I have to do, to receive everlasting life, is to believe in Jesus. As a matter of fact, many Television preachers conclude their broadcast asking their viewers to enter into such a prayer then claim that they believe that the viewer has now been saved.

James 2:19

Thou believest that there is one God; thou doest well: the devils also believe, and tremble.

This scripture in James, and the scripture we already covered in Matthew 7:21 would lead us to conclude that believing in Jesus is essential, but there must be more.

Let's look at a more detailed example of the need to read the entire bible for rightly dividing the truth.

The Four Accounts of the One True Gospel

Matthew 26:47-56

47 And while he yet spake, lo, Judas, one of the twelve, came, and with him a great multitude with swords and staves, from the chief priests and elders of the people.

BIBLE BONUS LESSON

48 Now he that betrayed him gave them a sign, saying, Whomsoever I shall kiss, that same is he: hold him fast.

49 And forthwith he came to Jesus, and said, Hail, master; and kissed him.

50 And Jesus said unto him, Friend, wherefore art thou come? Then came they, and laid hands on Jesus and took him.

51 And, behold, one of them which were with Jesus stretched out his hand, and drew his sword, and struck a servant of the high priest's, and smote off his ear.

52 Then said Jesus unto him, Put up again thy sword into his place: for all they that take the sword shall perish with the sword.

53 Thinkest thou that I cannot now pray to my Father, and he shall presently give me more than twelve legions of angels?

54 But how then shall the scriptures be fulfilled, that thus it must be?

55 In that same hour said Jesus to the multitudes, Are ye come out as against a thief with swords and staves for to take me? I sat daily with you teaching in the temple, and ye laid no hold on me.

56 But all this was done, that the scriptures of the prophets might be fulfilled. Then all the disciples forsook him, and fled.

BIBLE BONUS LESSON

Mark 14:44-50

44 And he that betrayed him had given them a token, saying, Whomsoever I shall kiss, that same is he; take him, and lead him away safely.

45 And as soon as he was come, he goeth straightway to him, and saith, Master, master; and kissed him.

46 And they laid their hands on him, and took him.

47 And one of them that stood by drew a sword, and smote a servant of the high priest, and cut off his ear.

48 And Jesus answered and said unto them, Are ye come out, as against a thief, with swords and with staves to take me?

49 I was daily with you in the temple teaching, and ye took me not: but the scriptures must be fulfilled.

50 And they all forsook him, and fled.

Luke 22:47-55

47 And while he yet spake, behold a multitude, and he that was called Judas, one of the twelve, went before them, and drew near unto Jesus to kiss him.

48 But Jesus said unto him, Judas, betrayest thou the Son of man with a kiss?

49 When they which were about him saw what would follow, they said unto him, Lord, shall we smite with the sword?

BIBLE BONUS LESSON

50 And one of them smote the servant of the high priest, and cut off his right ear.

51 And Jesus answered and said, Suffer ye thus far. And he touched his ear, and healed him.

52 Then Jesus said unto the chief priests, and captains of the temple, and the elders, which were come to him, Be ye come out, as against a thief, with swords and staves?

53 When I was daily with you in the temple, ye stretched forth no hands against me: but this is your hour, and the power of darkness.

54 Then took they him, and led him, and brought him into the high priest's house. And Peter followed afar off.

John 18:1-7 (KJV)

1 When Jesus had spoken these words, he went forth with his disciples over the brook Cedron, where was a garden, into the which he entered, and his disciples.

2 And Judas also, which betrayed him, knew the place: for Jesus ofttimes resorted thither with his disciples.

3 Judas then, having received a band of men and officers from the chief priests and Pharisees, cometh thither with lanterns and torches and weapons.

4 Jesus therefore, knowing all things that should come upon him, went forth, and said unto them, Whom seek ye?

BIBLE BONUS LESSON

5 They answered him, Jesus of Nazareth. Jesus saith unto them, I am he. And Judas also, which betrayed him, stood with them.

6 As soon then as he had said unto them, I am he, they went backward, and fell to the ground.

7 Then asked he them again, Whom seek ye? And they said, Jesus of Nazareth.

John 18:8-13

8 Jesus answered, I have told you that I am he: if therefore ye seek me, let these go their way:

9 That the saying might be fulfilled, which he spake, Of them which thou gavest me have I lost none.

10 Then Simon Peter having a sword drew it, and smote the high priest's servant, and cut off his right ear. The servant's name was Malchus.

11 Then said Jesus unto Peter, Put up thy sword into the sheath: the cup which my Father hath given me, shall I not drink it?

12 Then the band and the captain and officers of the Jews took Jesus, and bound him,

13 And led him away to Annas first; for he was father in law to Caiaphas, which was the high priest that same year.

BIBLE BONUS LESSON

Getting the whole picture...

The arrest of Jesus is the most well known arrest of all time. Every Easter, magazines and television stations broadcast the story of Jesus being arrested.

But for the story to be most complete, you have to read all four accounts of the one true Gospel.

Every topic in the Bible benefits from study. Many people read the Bible, but it takes study for a complete understanding of a particular topic.

Look at all the things we learn, from reading all four accounts of the arrest of Jesus Christ.

Matthew:

From Matthew's account we learn that Jesus has at his disposal, Twelve Legions of Angels. One read of the Old Testament lets us know Jesus would only need one angel to wipe out an entire Army. This not only gives us a glimpse of Jesus power, but shows us a demonstration of His restraint in using it.

Luke:

From Luke's account we learn that Jesus healed the high priests servant.

Matthew 5:44

44 But I say unto you, Love your enemies, bless them that curse you, do good to them that hate you, and pray for them which despitefully use you, and persecute you;

BIBLE BONUS LESSON

Here we see Jesus put into practice one of the more challenging of His instructions. Showing compassion for someone who means to do you harm. What do you think that servant would say, if later in life he was approached by someone who wanted to bad mouth Jesus?

As much as the media and enemies bad mouth Christianity, they usually avoid bad mouthing Jesus.

This account also shows Jesus responds to Judas kiss of betrayal. No matter how much planning and scheming you do, you will never out smart God.

Galatians 6:7

Be not deceived; God is not mocked: for whatsoever a man soweth, that shall he also reap.

Peter followed. So not all fled. Over and over I hear preachers single out Peter as the hot headed buffoon of the Apostles. Yes Peter would later crack under the pressure, but he rose up to defend his Lord and he stayed when others ran.

John:

While other accounts state that Jesus followers fled. John's account shows us that Jesus was in agreement with them leaving Him. Jesus demonstrated His agreement by stepping forward multiple times to identify Himself and by asking for the soldiers to "let these go their way." In a time when CEOs and politicians and other leaders seek to blame others for their problems, this is an amazing demonstration of leadership.

BIBLE BONUS LESSON

Facing death and taking responsibility.

As soon as Jesus spoke, they went backwards and fell to the ground. Rarely is this amazing part of Jesus arrest portrayed. Another demonstration of Jesus's power and His restraint in using it. We also get another glimpse of the power of the tongue.

When Jesus spoke with Satan, He repeatedly spoke the word of God. That word repelled the Devil.

We can repel a great deal of pain in our life by speaking the word of God.

John's account is also the only account that tells us it was Peter who drew his sword and that Malchus was the name of the servant who was injured and healed.

Better Understanding

By reading all four accounts we have a deeper, richer understanding of the power and love of Jesus.

<u>The Power</u>

* Just by speaking the soldiers fell backwards.

* 12 Legions of Angels at His disposal.

- Jesus healed His enemy with just 1 touch.

-

BIBLE BONUS LESSON

<u>The Love</u>

* Jesus stepped forward to save His followers.

* Jesus allowed His followers to leave.

* Jesus acknowledged Judas betrayal without retribution.

* Jesus wanted the will of the Father fulfilled

PART 4
NEW TESTAMENT BIBLE VERSES: HISTORY & THE EPISTLES

NT BIBLE VERSES: HISTORY & THE EPISTLES

History, the book of ACTS

Acts 4:12

12 Neither is there salvation in any other: for there is none other name under heaven given among men, whereby we must be saved.

Acts 7:49

49 Heaven is my throne, and earth is my footstool: what house will ye build me? saith the Lord: or what is the place of my rest?

Acts 1:11

11 Which also said, Ye men of Galilee, why stand ye gazing up into heaven? this same Jesus, which is taken up from you into heaven, shall so come in like manner as ye have seen him go into heaven.

NT BIBLE VERSES: HISTORY & THE EPISTLES

The Epistles

Romans 6:23

23 For the wages of sin is death; but the gift of God is eternal life through Jesus Christ our Lord.

Romans 1:18

18 For the wrath of God is revealed from heaven against all ungodliness and unrighteousness of men, who hold the truth in unrighteousness;

Romans 5:17

17 For if by one man's offence death reigned by one; much more they which receive abundance of grace and of the gift of righteousness shall reign in life by one, Jesus Christ.

NT BIBLE VERSES: HISTORY & THE EPISTLES

7. Romans 10:9-13

9 That if thou shalt confess with thy mouth the Lord Jesus, and shalt believe in thine heart that God hath raised him from the dead, thou shalt be saved.

10 For with the heart man believeth unto righteousness; and with the mouth confession is made unto salvation.

11 For the scripture saith, Whosoever believeth on him shall not be ashamed.

12 For there is no difference between the Jew and the Greek: for the same Lord over all is rich unto all that call upon him.

13 For whosoever shall call upon the name of the Lord shall be saved.

3. 1 Corinthians 2:9

9 But as it is written, Eye hath not seen, nor ear heard, neither have entered into the heart of man, the things which God hath prepared for them that love him.

NT BIBLE VERSES: HISTORY & THE EPISTLES

1 Corinthians 6:9-11

9 Know ye not that the unrighteous shall not inherit the kingdom of God? Be not deceived: neither fornicators, nor idolaters, nor adulterers, nor effeminate, nor abusers of themselves with mankind,

10 Nor thieves, nor covetous, nor drunkards, nor revilers, nor extortioners, shall inherit the kingdom of God.

11 And such were some of you: but ye are washed, but ye are sanctified, but ye are justified in the name of the Lord Jesus, and by the Spirit of our God.

1 Corinthians 15:51-52

51 Behold, I shew you a mystery; We shall not all sleep, but we shall all be changed,

52 In a moment, in the twinkling of an eye, at the last trump: for the trumpet shall sound, and the dead shall be raised incorruptible, and we shall be changed.

NT BIBLE VERSES: HISTORY & THE EPISTLES

2 Corinthians 5:1

For we know that if our earthly house of this tabernacle were dissolved, we have a building of God, an house not made with hands, eternal in the heavens.

2 Corinthians 5:8

8 We are confident, I say, and willing rather to be absent from the body, and to be present with the Lord.

2 Corinthians 12:2

2 I knew a man in Christ above fourteen years ago, (whether in the body, I cannot tell; or whether out of the body, I cannot tell: God knoweth;) such an one caught up to the third heaven.

Ephesians 1:18

18 The eyes of your understanding being enlightened; that ye may know what is the hope of his calling, and what the riches of the glory of his inheritance in the saints,

NT BIBLE VERSES: HISTORY & THE EPISTLES

Ephesians 2:8-9

8 For by grace are ye saved through faith; and that not of yourselves: it is the gift of God:

9 Not of works, lest any man should boast.

Ephesians 5:1-7

Be ye therefore followers of God, as dear children;

2 And walk in love, as Christ also hath loved us, and hath given himself for us an offering and a sacrifice to God for a sweet smelling savour.

3 But fornication, and all uncleanness, or covetousness, let it not be once named among you, as becometh saints;

4 Neither filthiness, nor foolish talking, nor jesting, which are not convenient: but rather giving of thanks.

5 For this ye know, that no whoremonger, nor unclean person, nor covetous man, who is an idolater, hath any inheritance in the kingdom of Christ and of God.

NT BIBLE VERSES: HISTORY & THE EPISTLES

6 Let no man deceive you with vain words: for because of these things cometh the wrath of God upon the children of disobedience.

7 Be not ye therefore partakers with them.

Colossians 1:12

12 Giving thanks unto the Father, which hath made us meet to be partakers of the inheritance of the saints in light:

Colossians 3:1-7

If ye then be risen with Christ, seek those things which are above, where Christ sitteth on the right hand of God.

2 Set your affection on things above, not on things on the earth.

3 For ye are dead, and your life is hid with Christ in God.
4 When Christ, who is our life, shall appear, then shall ye also appear with him in glory.

NT BIBLE VERSES: HISTORY & THE EPISTLES

5 Mortify therefore your members which are upon the earth; fornication, uncleanness, inordinate affection, evil concupiscence, and covetousness, which is idolatry:

6 For which things' sake the wrath of God cometh on the children of disobedience:

7 In the which ye also walked some time, when ye lived in them.

9. Hebrews 11:16

16 But now they desire a better country, that is, an heavenly: wherefore God is not ashamed to be called their God: for he hath prepared for them a city.

Hebrews 13:14

14 For here have we no continuing city, but we seek one to come.

NT BIBLE VERSES: HISTORY & THE EPISTLES

Hebrews 11:10

10 For he looked for a city which hath foundations, whose builder and maker is God.

Hebrews 12:22-24

22 But ye are come unto mount Sion, and unto the city of the living God, the heavenly Jerusalem, and to an innumerable company of angels,

23 To the general assembly and church of the firstborn, which are written in heaven, and to God the Judge of all, and to the spirits of just men made perfect,

24 And to Jesus the mediator of the new covenant, and to the blood of sprinkling, that speaketh better things than that of Abel.

Philippians 3:20-21

20 For our conversation is in heaven; from whence also we look for the Saviour, the Lord Jesus Christ:

NT BIBLE VERSES: HISTORY & THE EPISTLES

21 Who shall change our vile body, that it may be fashioned like unto his glorious body, according to the working whereby he is able even to subdue all things unto himself.

1 Peter 1:4

4 To an inheritance incorruptible, and undefiled, and that fadeth not away, reserved in heaven for you,

10. 2 Peter 3:13

13 Nevertheless we, according to his promise, look for new heavens and a new earth, wherein dwelleth righteousness.

2 Peter 3:10

10 But the day of the Lord will come as a thief in the night; in the which the heavens shall pass away with a great noise, and the elements shall melt with fervent heat, the earth also and the works that are therein shall be burned up.

NT BIBLE VERSES: HISTORY & THE EPISTLES

1 Timothy 6:17-19

17 Charge them that are rich in this world, that they be not highminded, nor trust in uncertain riches, but in the living God, who giveth us richly all things to enjoy;

18 That they do good, that they be rich in good works, ready to distribute, willing to communicate;

19 Laying up in store for themselves a good foundation against the time to come, that they may lay hold on eternal life.

Galatians 5:19-25

19 Now the works of the flesh are manifest, which are these; Adultery, fornication, uncleanness, lasciviousness,

20 Idolatry, witchcraft, hatred, variance, emulations, wrath, strife, seditions, heresies,

21 Envyings, murders, drunkenness, revellings, and such like: of the which I tell you before, as I have also told you in time past, that they which do such things shall not inherit the kingdom of God.

NT BIBLE VERSES: HISTORY & THE EPISTLES

22 But the fruit of the Spirit is love, joy, peace, longsuffering, gentleness, goodness, faith,

23 Meekness, temperance: against such there is no law.

24 And they that are Christ's have crucified the flesh with the affections and lusts.

25 If we live in the Spirit, let us also walk in the Spirit.

1 Thessalonians 4:13-18

13 But I would not have you to be ignorant, brethren, concerning them which are asleep, that ye sorrow not, even as others which have no hope.

14 For if we believe that Jesus died and rose again, even so them also which sleep in Jesus will God bring with him.

15 For this we say unto you by the word of the Lord, that we which are alive and remain unto the coming of the Lord shall not prevent them which are asleep.

NT BIBLE VERSES: HISTORY & THE EPISTLES

16 For the Lord himself shall descend from heaven with a shout, with the voice of the archangel, and with the trump of God: and the dead in Christ shall rise first:

17 Then we which are alive and remain shall be caught up together with them in the clouds, to meet the Lord in the air: and so shall we ever be with the Lord.

18 Wherefore comfort one another with these words.

1 John 3:2

2 Beloved, now are we the sons of God, and it doth not yet appear what we shall be: but we know that, when he shall appear, we shall be like him; for we shall see him as he is.

1 John 5:5-8

5 Who is he that overcometh the world, but he that believeth that Jesus is the Son of God?

NT BIBLE VERSES: HISTORY & THE EPISTLES

6 This is he that came by water and blood, even Jesus Christ; not by water only, but by water and blood. And it is the Spirit that beareth witness, because the Spirit is truth.

7 For there are three that bear record in heaven, the Father, the Word, and the Holy Ghost: and these three are one.

8 And there are three that bear witness in earth, the Spirit, and the water, and the blood: and these three agree in one.

BIBLE BONUS LESSON: Do Not Add To or Take Away

BIBLE BONUS LESSON

IV. Do not add to or take away.

Deuteronomy 4:2

Ye shall not add unto the word which I command you, neither shall ye diminish ought from it, that ye may keep the commandments of the Lord your God which I command you.

Proverbs 30:5-6

5 Every word of God is pure: he is a shield unto them that put their trust in him.

6 Add thou not unto his words, lest he reprove thee, and thou be found a liar.

Revelation 22:18-19

18 For I testify unto every man that heareth the words of the prophecy of this book, If any man shall add unto these things, God shall add unto him the plagues that are written in this book:

19 And if any man shall take away from the words of the book of this prophecy, God shall take away his part out of the book of life, and out of the holy city, and from the things which are written in this book.

In the beginning, the middle and the end of the Bible the message is consistent. Do not add or take away from the word of God.

BIBLE BONUS LESSON

Often some of the biggest misunderstandings arise when the doctrine of men is added to the word of God.

2 Timothy 3:16-17

16 All scripture is given by inspiration of God, and is profitable for doctrine, for reproof, for correction, for instruction in righteousness:

17 That the man of God may be perfect, thoroughly furnished unto all good works.

If you can be perfect, thoroughly furnished for all, not some, but all good works, why would a church or religion need to create doctrine that is a addition to the word of God?

Mark 7:1-5

1 Then came together unto him the Pharisees, and certain of the scribes, which came from Jerusalem.

2 And when they saw some of his disciples eat bread with defiled, that is to say, with unwashen, hands, they found fault.

3 For the Pharisees, and all the Jews, except they wash their hands oft, eat not, holding the tradition of the elders.

4 And when they come from the market, except they wash, they eat not. And many other things there be, which they have received to hold, as the washing of cups, and pots, brasen vessels, and of tables.

BIBLE BONUS LESSON

5 Then the Pharisees and scribes asked him, Why walk not thy disciples according to the tradition of the elders, but eat bread with unwashen hands?

Mark 7:6-9

6 He answered and said unto them, Well hath Esaias prophesied of you hypocrites, as it is written, This people honoureth me with their lips, but their heart is far from me.

7 Howbeit in vain do they worship me, teaching for doctrines the commandments of men.

8 For laying aside the commandment of God, ye hold the tradition of men, as the washing of pots and cups: and many other such like things ye do.

9 And he said unto them, Full well ye reject the commandment of God, that ye may keep your own tradition.

Be like the Bereans in Acts 17. Search the scriptures and validate any doctrine or tradition with the word of God.

Vain: producing no result; useless.

Jesus called their worship vain. Useless. This is how one can end up like the lost believer Jesus describes in Matthew 7:21. Study the word of God and insure that your worship is the word of God not the doctrine of men.

BIBLE BONUS LESSON

Tips on Reading the Entire Bible Quickly

It takes approximately 90 hours to read the entire Bible.

I realize many of us have very busy lives, but consider this. God gives you 168 hours each and every week. Yet He asks so little in return.

Purchase a audio book version of the Bible and listen to it when you are driving your car. Many people have head phones on while working out at a gym, running or even at work. So if you truly desire to learn more, you can make it so.

Download a audio version of the Bible onto your personal computer and listen when you are online.

Cut out one Television program per day or week. Eliminate time thieves like long phone or unplanned conversations. Let your phone take the call and call back after you have finished your study.

PART 5
NEW TESTAMENT BIBLE VERSES: PROPHECY

NT BIBLE VERSES: PROPHECY

The book of Revelation

Revelation 5:9

9 And they sung a new song, saying, Thou art worthy to take the book, and to open the seals thereof: for thou wast slain, and hast redeemed us to God by thy blood out of every kindred, and tongue, and people, and nation;

Revelation 2:7

7 He that hath an ear, let him hear what the Spirit saith unto the churches; To him that overcometh will I give to eat of the tree of life, which is in the midst of the paradise of God.

Revelation 7:9

9 After this I beheld, and, lo, a great multitude, which no man could number, of all nations, and kindreds, and people, and tongues, stood before the throne, and before the Lamb, clothed with white robes, and palms in their hands;

NT BIBLE VERSES: PROPHECY

Revelation 14:13

13 And I heard a voice from heaven saying unto me, Write, Blessed are the dead which die in the Lord from henceforth: Yea, saith the Spirit, that they may rest from their labours; and their works do follow them.

Revelation 11:19

19 And the temple of God was opened in heaven, and there was seen in his temple the ark of his testament: and there were lightnings, and voices, and thunderings, and an earthquake, and great hail.

Revelation 20:11

11 And I saw a great white throne, and him that sat on it, from whose face the earth and the heaven fled away; and there was found no place for them.

NT BIBLE VERSES: PROPHECY

Revelation 12:7-9

7 And there was war in heaven: Michael and his angels fought against the dragon; and the dragon fought and his angels,

8 And prevailed not; neither was their place found any more in heaven.

9 And the great dragon was cast out, that old serpent, called the Devil, and Satan, which deceiveth the whole world: he was cast out into the earth, and his angels were cast out with him.

Revelation 22:15

15 For without are dogs, and sorcerers, and whoremongers, and murderers, and idolaters, and whosoever loveth and maketh a lie.

NT BIBLE VERSES: PROPHECY

Revelation 7:13-17

13 And one of the elders answered, saying unto me, What are these which are arrayed in white robes? and whence came they?

14 And I said unto him, Sir, thou knowest. And he said to me, These are they which came out of great tribulation, and have washed their robes, and made them white in the blood of the Lamb.

15 Therefore are they before the throne of God, and serve him day and night in his temple: and he that sitteth on the throne shall dwell among them.

16 They shall hunger no more, neither thirst any more; neither shall the sun light on them, nor any heat.

17 For the Lamb which is in the midst of the throne shall feed them, and shall lead them unto living fountains of waters: and God shall wipe away all tears from their eyes.

NT BIBLE VERSES: PROPHECY

Revelation 4:1-11

After this I looked, and, behold, a door was opened in heaven: and the first voice which I heard was as it were of a trumpet talking with me; which said, Come up hither, and I will shew thee things which must be hereafter.

2 And immediately I was in the spirit: and, behold, a throne was set in heaven, and one sat on the throne.

3 And he that sat was to look upon like a jasper and a sardine stone: and there was a rainbow round about the throne, in sight like unto an emerald.

4 And round about the throne were four and twenty seats: and upon the seats I saw four and twenty elders sitting, clothed in white raiment; and they had on their heads crowns of gold.

5 And out of the throne proceeded lightnings and thunderings and voices: and there were seven lamps of fire burning before the throne, which are the seven Spirits of God.

NT BIBLE VERSES: PROPHECY

6 And before the throne there was a sea of glass like unto crystal: and in the midst of the throne, and round about the throne, were four beasts full of eyes before and behind.

7 And the first beast was like a lion, and the second beast like a calf, and the third beast had a face as a man, and the fourth beast was like a flying eagle.

8 And the four beasts had each of them six wings about him; and they were full of eyes within: and they rest not day and night, saying, Holy, holy, holy, Lord God Almighty, which was, and is, and is to come.

9 And when those beasts give glory and honour and thanks to him that sat on the throne, who liveth for ever and ever,

10 The four and twenty elders fall down before him that sat on the throne, and worship him that liveth for ever and ever, and cast their crowns before the throne, saying,

NT BIBLE VERSES: PROPHECY

11 Thou art worthy, O Lord, to receive glory and honour and power: for thou hast created all things, and for thy pleasure they are and were created.

Revelation 21:1-27

And I saw a new heaven and a new earth: for the first heaven and the first earth were passed away; and there was no more sea.

2 And I John saw the holy city, new Jerusalem, coming down from God out of heaven, prepared as a bride adorned for her husband.

3 And I heard a great voice out of heaven saying, Behold, the tabernacle of God is with men, and he will dwell with them, and they shall be his people, and God himself shall be with them, and be their God.

4 And God shall wipe away all tears from their eyes; and there shall be no more death, neither sorrow, nor crying, neither shall there be any more pain: for the former things are passed away.

NT BIBLE VERSES: PROPHECY

5 And he that sat upon the throne said, Behold, I make all things new. And he said unto me, Write: for these words are true and faithful.

6 And he said unto me, It is done. I am Alpha and Omega, the beginning and the end. I will give unto him that is athirst of the fountain of the water of life freely.

7 He that overcometh shall inherit all things; and I will be his God, and he shall be my son.

8 But the fearful, and unbelieving, and the abominable, and murderers, and whoremongers, and sorcerers, and idolaters, and all liars, shall have their part in the lake which burneth with fire and brimstone: which is the second death.

9 And there came unto me one of the seven angels which had the seven vials full of the seven last plagues, and talked with me, saying, Come hither, I will shew thee the bride, the Lamb's wife.

NT BIBLE VERSES: PROPHECY

10 And he carried me away in the spirit to a great and high mountain, and shewed me that great city, the holy Jerusalem, descending out of heaven from God,

11 Having the glory of God: and her light was like unto a stone most precious, even like a jasper stone, clear as crystal;

12 And had a wall great and high, and had twelve gates, and at the gates twelve angels, and names written thereon, which are the names of the twelve tribes of the children of Israel:

13 On the east three gates; on the north three gates; on the south three gates; and on the west three gates.

14 And the wall of the city had twelve foundations, and in them the names of the twelve apostles of the Lamb.

15 And he that talked with me had a golden reed to measure the city, and the gates thereof, and the wall thereof.

NT BIBLE VERSES: PROPHECY

16 And the city lieth foursquare, and the length is as large as the breadth: and he measured the city with the reed, twelve thousand furlongs. The length and the breadth and the height of it are equal.

17 And he measured the wall thereof, an hundred and forty and four cubits, according to the measure of a man, that is, of the angel.

18 And the building of the wall of it was of jasper: and the city was pure gold, like unto clear glass.

19 And the foundations of the wall of the city were garnished with all manner of precious stones. The first foundation was jasper; the second, sapphire; the third, a chalcedony; the fourth, an emerald;

20 The fifth, sardonyx; the sixth, sardius; the seventh, chrysolyte; the eighth, beryl; the ninth, a topaz; the tenth, a chrysoprasus; the eleventh, a jacinth; the twelfth, an amethyst.

NT BIBLE VERSES: PROPHECY

21 And the twelve gates were twelve pearls: every several gate was of one pearl: and the street of the city was pure gold, as it were transparent glass.

22 And I saw no temple therein: for the Lord God Almighty and the Lamb are the temple of it.

23 And the city had no need of the sun, neither of the moon, to shine in it: for the glory of God did lighten it, and the Lamb is the light thereof.

24 And the nations of them which are saved shall walk in the light of it: and the kings of the earth do bring their glory and honour into it.

25 And the gates of it shall not be shut at all by day: for there shall be no night there.

26 And they shall bring the glory and honour of the nations into it.

NT BIBLE VERSES: PROPHECY

27 And there shall in no wise enter into it any thing that defileth, neither whatsoever worketh abomination, or maketh a lie: but they which are written in the Lamb's book of life.

Revelation 22:1-5

And he shewed me a pure river of water of life, clear as crystal, proceeding out of the throne of God and of the Lamb.

2 In the midst of the street of it, and on either side of the river, was there the tree of life, which bare twelve manner of fruits, and yielded her fruit every month: and the leaves of the tree were for the healing of the nations.

3 And there shall be no more curse: but the throne of God and of the Lamb shall be in it; and his servants shall serve him:

4 And they shall see his face; and his name shall be in their foreheads.

NT BIBLE VERSES: PROPHECY

5 And there shall be no night there; and they need no candle, neither light of the sun; for the Lord God giveth them light: and they shall reign for ever and ever.

Revelation 21:4

4 And God shall wipe away all tears from their eyes; and there shall be no more death, neither sorrow, nor crying, neither shall there be any more pain: for the former things are passed away.

BIBLE BONUS LESSON: Faith Without Works is Dead

BIBLE BONUS LESSON

V. Faith without works is dead.

Luke 6:46

And why call ye me, Lord, Lord, and do not the things which I say?

James 1:22

But be ye doers of the word, and not hearers only, deceiving your own selves.

James 2:26

For as the body without the spirit is dead, so faith without works is dead also.

Revelation 3:15-16

15 I know thy works, that thou art neither cold nor hot: I would thou wert cold or hot.

16 So then because thou art lukewarm, and neither cold nor hot, I will spue thee out of my mouth.

 Psalm 1

1 Blessed is the man that walketh not in the counsel of the ungodly, nor standeth in the way of sinners, nor sitteth in the seat of the scornful.

2 But his delight is in the law of the Lord; and in his law doth he meditate day and night.

BIBLE BONUS LESSON

3 And he shall be like a tree planted by the rivers of water, that bringeth forth his fruit in his season; his leaf also shall not wither; and whatsoever he doeth shall prosper.

"Whatsoever he doeth shall Prosper"

You meditate day and night on the word and then you do something, take action. You will understand the word of God better when you put it into practice.

How many things where you taught in school, even got passing grades, but because of lack of repetition you no longer remember?

Teaching another, individually or a class is a great way to reinforce what you study.

PART 6
BIBLE LIFE LESSON: MATTHEW CHAPTER 7

Bible Life Lesson for Heaven: Matthew Chapter 7

Judge not, that ye be not judged.

2 For with what judgment ye judge, ye shall be judged: and with what measure ye mete, it shall be measured to you again.

3 And why beholdest thou the mote that is in thy brother's eye, but considerest not the beam that is in thine own eye?

4 Or how wilt thou say to thy brother, Let me pull out the mote out of thine eye; and, behold, a beam is in thine own eye?

5 Thou hypocrite, first cast out the beam out of thine own eye; and then shalt thou see clearly to cast out the mote out of thy brother's eye.

6 Give not that which is holy unto the dogs, neither cast ye your pearls before swine, lest they trample them under their feet, and turn again and rend you.

Bible Life Lesson for Heaven: Matthew Chapter 7

7 Ask, and it shall be given you; seek, and ye shall find; knock, and it shall be opened unto you:

8 For every one that asketh receiveth; and he that seeketh findeth; and to him that knocketh it shall be opened.

9 Or what man is there of you, whom if his son ask bread, will he give him a stone?

10 Or if he ask a fish, will he give him a serpent?

11 If ye then, being evil, know how to give good gifts unto your children, how much more shall your Father which is in heaven give good things to them that ask him?

12 Therefore all things whatsoever ye would that men should do to you, do ye even so to them: for this is the law and the prophets.

13 Enter ye in at the strait gate: for wide is the gate, and broad is the way, that leadeth to destruction, and many there be which go in thereat:

Bible Life Lesson for Heaven: Matthew Chapter 7

14 Because strait is the gate, and narrow is the way, which leadeth unto life, and few there be that find it.

15 Beware of false prophets, which come to you in sheep's clothing, but inwardly they are ravening wolves.

16 Ye shall know them by their fruits. Do men gather grapes of thorns, or figs of thistles?

17 Even so every good tree bringeth forth good fruit; but a corrupt tree bringeth forth evil fruit.

18 A good tree cannot bring forth evil fruit, neither can a corrupt tree bring forth good fruit.

19 Every tree that bringeth not forth good fruit is hewn down, and cast into the fire.

20 Wherefore by their fruits ye shall know them.

21 Not every one that saith unto me, Lord, Lord, shall enter into the kingdom of heaven; but he that doeth the will of my Father which is in heaven.

Bible Life Lesson for Heaven: Matthew Chapter 7

22 Many will say to me in that day, Lord, Lord, have we not prophesied in thy name? and in thy name have cast out devils? and in thy name done many wonderful works?

23 And then will I profess unto them, I never knew you: depart from me, ye that work iniquity.

24 Therefore whosoever heareth these sayings of mine, and doeth them, I will liken him unto a wise man, which built his house upon a rock:

25 And the rain descended, and the floods came, and the winds blew, and beat upon that house; and it fell not: for it was founded upon a rock.

26 And every one that heareth these sayings of mine, and doeth them not, shall be likened unto a foolish man, which built his house upon the sand:

27 And the rain descended, and **the floods came**, and the winds blew, and beat upon that house; and it fell: and great was the fall of it.

Bible Life Lesson for Heaven: Matthew Chapter 7

28 And it came to pass, when Jesus had ended these sayings, the people were astonished at his doctrine:

29 For he taught them as one having authority, and not as the scribes.

Matthew chapter 7 is easily my favorite chapter in the bible. There is a lot to unpack from this chapter, so lets start with a few key take aways.

Matthew 7:1

* Be less judgemental. There is a difference between telling someone what the bible says and passing a judgement along the way. If you are speaking the word of God, the judgement has already been passed by God.

Matthew 7:5

* We should be careful to get our house in order before looking to clean up another's mess.

Matthew 7:11

* Don't be afraid to ask God for what you want. God wants to bless you the same as you enjoy blessing your children/friends or family members.

Bible Life Lesson for Heaven: Matthew Chapter 7

Matthew 7:14

* There were only a few people that made it to safety in Noah's time. There will be few that find the path to Heaven.

Matthew 7:20

* The best way to determine what kind of person you are dealing with is to watch their consistant actions. By their fruits you shall know them.

Matthew 7:21-27

- You can believe in Jesus, do many works in His name and still be rejected. Jesus stated "I NEVER knew you" this could be interpreted that this person never properly obeyed the Gospel. You must confess before man, not at home watching your TV sermons. You must be baptized for the remission of sins, you must remain faithful unto death (Revelation 2:10). You must do what the Lord says. Luke 6:46. How important is it that you do exactly what God says..? please read about Naaman the leper in 2 Kings 5.

-

Bible Life Lesson for Heaven: Matthew Chapter 7

* Notice that the floods came to both the person who obeyed God as well as the one who did not. So our life will always be full of challenges. However the house that was build on a solid foundation withstood the storm. Our actions before, during and after can help determine how servere those challenges are.

Jesus was in the wilderness for 40 days. The children of Israel were wandering around for 40 years.

Revelation 3:16 let's us know that even if we are in the body, we can be removed, if we decide to go on spiritual cruise control.

All sin and fall short of the glory of God. However what you do about that sin makes all the difference to

God. King Saul pretended the sin did not happen. He was removed as king.

King David acknowledge the sin and repented. He was punished, but remained king and later would be described in the book of Acts as a man after God's own heart. (Acts 13:22)

Peter denied Jesus. Even cursed up a storm. But Jesus forgave him. And He will forgive you.

PART 7
TOP 10 BIBLE VERSES ABOUT HEAVEN

TOP 10 BIBLE VERSES ABOUT HEAVEN

Here is the top 10 list of bible verses on Heaven as voted on by Christians around the world

10. 2 Peter 3:13

13 Nevertheless we, according to his promise, look for new heavens and a new earth, wherein dwelleth righteousness.

9. Hebrews 11:16

16 But now they desire a better country, that is, an heavenly: wherefore God is not ashamed to be called their God: for he hath prepared for them a city.

8. Matthew 6:19-21

19 Lay not up for yourselves treasures upon earth, where moth and rust doth corrupt, and where thieves break through and steal:

TOP 10 BIBLE VERSES ABOUT HEAVEN

20 But lay up for yourselves treasures in heaven, where neither moth nor rust doth corrupt, and where thieves do not break through nor steal:

21 For where your treasure is, there will your heart be also.

7. Romans 10:9-13

9 That if thou shalt confess with thy mouth the Lord Jesus, and shalt believe in thine heart that God hath raised him from the dead, thou shalt be saved.

10 For with the heart man believeth unto righteousness; and with the mouth confession is made unto salvation.

11 For the scripture saith, Whosoever believeth on him shall not be ashamed.

12 For there is no difference between the Jew and the Greek: for the same Lord over all is rich unto all that call upon him.

TOP 10 BIBLE VERSES ABOUT HEAVEN

13 For whosoever shall call upon the name of the Lord shall be saved.

6. Luke 23:43

43 And Jesus said unto him, Verily I say unto thee, Today shalt thou be with me in paradise.

5. Revelation 22:1-5

And he shewed me a pure river of water of life, clear as crystal, proceeding out of the throne of God and of the Lamb.

2 In the midst of the street of it, and on either side of the river, was there the tree of life, which bare twelve manner of fruits, and yielded her fruit every month: and the leaves of the tree were for the healing of the nations.

3 And there shall be no more curse: but the throne of God and of the Lamb shall be in it; and his servants shall serve him:

TOP 10 BIBLE VERSES ABOUT HEAVEN

4 And they shall see his face; and his name shall be in their foreheads.

5 And there shall be no night there; and they need no candle, neither light of the sun; for the Lord God giveth them light: and they shall reign for ever and ever.

4. John 3:16

16 For God so loved the world, that he gave his only begotten Son, that whosoever believeth in him should not perish, but have everlasting life.

3. 1 Corinthians 2:9

9 But as it is written, Eye hath not seen, nor ear heard, neither have entered into the heart of man, the things which God hath prepared for them that love him.

2. John 14:2

2 In my Father's house are many mansions: if it were not so, I would have told you. I go to prepare a place for you.

TOP 10 BIBLE VERSES ABOUT HEAVEN

1. Revelation 21:4

4 And God shall wipe away all tears from their eyes; and there shall be no more death, neither sorrow, nor crying, neither shall there be any more pain: for the former things are passed away.

A few questions about the top 10 bible verses about Heaven.

Do you agree?

Do you have a scripture that you believe should be in the top 10? If so, why?

How do these top 10 scriptures make you feel about Heaven?

Are you excited? Are you afraid?

How do you think God wants you to feel about Heaven?

Either way we should get comfortable about Heaven. Because we have an appointment that none of us are going to miss.

TOP 10 BIBLE VERSES ABOUT HEAVEN

Hebrews 9:27

And as it is appointed unto men once to die, but after this the judgment:

PART 8
BIBLE QUIZ ON HEAVEN

BIBLE QUIZ ON HEAVEN

Welcome to the quiz on bible verses about Heaven. You are going to have ten questions, at least one from each section of the entire book.

1. Which bible verse says that God created the Heavens and the Earth?

a. Genesis 1:1
b. Isaiah 65:17
c. Isaiah 45:18
d. All of the above

2. Which bible verse says that Elijah went up by a whirlwind into heaven?

a. I Kings 2:11
b. 2 Kings 2:11
c. Matthew 2:11
d. Isaiah 2:11

3. What bible verse says:
"Lay not up for yourselves treasures upon earth, where moth and rust doth corrupt, and where thieves break through and steal:"

a. Matthew 6:19
b. Matthew 7:19
c. Mark 7:19
d. Luke 7:19

BIBLE QUIZ ON HEAVEN

4. What bible verse says:
"Neither is there salvation in any other: for there is none other name under heaven given among men, whereby we must be saved."

a. Matthew 4:12
b. Mark 4:12
c. Acts 4:12
d. Jude 4:12

5. What bible verse says:
" And I saw a great white throne, and him that sat on it, from whose face the earth and the heaven fled away; and there was found no place for them."

a. 1 Thessalonians 3:11
b. 2 Thessalonians 2:11
c. Revelation 3:16
d. Revelation 20:11

6. Which Bible Verse was voted the number 2 bible verse on Heaven?

a. Revelation 21:4
b. John 14:2
c. John 3:16
d. Genesis 1:1

7. Which Bible Verse was voted the number 1 bible verse on Heaven?

a. Matthew 21:4
b. Revelation 1:1
c. Hebrews 11:1
d. Revelation 21:4

BIBLE QUIZ ON HEAVEN

8. Fill in the blank:
"Or how wilt thou say to thy brother, Let me pull out the mote out of thine eye; and, behold, a _____ is in thine _____ _____?"

a. "a mote is in thine own eye ?"
b. "a sin is in thine own eye ?"
c. "a beam is in thine own eye?"
d. "a board is in thine right eye ?"

9. How will you know that a person is evil if they seem like a nice person?

a. You must pray to God, to reveal the true nature of anyone you meet.
b. The power of life and death is in the tongue, go by what they say.
c. Matthew 12:34 O generation of vipers, how can ye, being evil, speak good things? for out of the abundance of the heart the mouth speaketh.
d. Observe their consistent actions

10. How could someone call on the Lord, and do many wonderful works in the name of the Lord yet be told to "depart from me, ye that work iniquity."

a. Luke 6:46
b. Matthew 7:26
c. Matthew 7:23
d. All of the above

ANSWERS

1. Which bible verse says that God created the Heavens and the Earth?

d. All of the above

2. Which bible verse says that Elijah went up by a whirlwind into heaven?

b. 2 Kings 2:11

3. What bible verse says:
"Lay not up for yourselves treasures upon earth, where moth and rust doth corrupt, and where thieves break through and steal:"

a. Matthew 6:19

4. What bible verse says:
 "Neither is there salvation in any other: for there is none other name under heaven given among men, whereby we must be saved."

c. Acts 4:12

5. What bible verse says:
" And I saw a great white throne, and him that sat on it, from whose face the earth and the heaven fled away; and there was found no place for them."

d. Revelation 20:11

6. Which Bible Verse was voted the number 2 bible verse on Heaven?

b. John 14:2

ANSWERS

7. Which Bible Verse was voted the number 1 bible verse on Heaven?

d. Revelation 21:4

8. Fill in the blank:
"Or how wilt thou say to thy brother, Let me pull out the mote out of thine eye; and, behold, a _____ is in thine _____ _____?"

c. a beam is in thine own eye?"

9. How will you know that a person is evil if they seem like a nice person?

d. Observe their consistent actions

Matthew 7:20 Wherefore by their fruits ye shall know them.

10. How could someone call on the Lord, and do many wonderful works in the name of the Lord yet be told to "depart from me, ye that work iniquity."

d. All of the above

If you got all of the questions right, congratulations! If not, then continue to study you will get better!

2 Timothy 2:15

Study to shew thyself approved unto God, a workman that needeth not to be ashamed, rightly dividing the word of truth.

CONCLUSION

CONCLUSION

I want to thank you for completing this book.
Now you have the knowledge of...

* The best Old Testament Bible Verses on **Heaven**!
* The best New Testament Bible Verses on **Heaven**!
* The top 10 Scriptures on **Heaven**
* Knowledge of an Amazing Bible story or scriptures that do a great job to best illustrate **Heaven** principles
* An elevated knowledge of your understanding of this amazing Bible topic!

You have taken a step forward to being ready to give an answer to every man that asketh you a reason for the hope that is in you.... **1 Peter 3:15**

You have taken the time to grow spiritually so you can share the good news of Jesus the Christ and the Word of God.

Romans 10:17

So then faith cometh by hearing, and hearing by the word of God.

You have increased your faith!

CONCLUSION

But don't let this be the end! Be like those in Berea...

Acts 17:10-11

10 And the brethren immediately sent away Paul and Silas by night unto Berea: who coming thither went into the synagogue of the Jews.

11 These were more noble than those in Thessalonica, in that they received the word with all readiness of mind, and searched the scriptures daily, whether those things were so.

This is only one of what will be a 40 book ibrary of books covering the many fascinating topics in the Bible.

Thanks again...and may God continue to guide, guard and protect you and yours.

Now let me leave you with this encouraging scripture about the power of receiving the word of God both day and night.

CONCLUSION

Psalm 1:1-3

1 Blessed is the man that walketh not in the counsel of the ungodly, nor standeth in the way of sinners, nor sitteth in the seat of the scornful.

2 But his delight is in the law of the Lord; and in his law doth he meditate day and night.

3 And he shall be like a tree planted by the rivers of water, that bringeth forth his fruit in his season; his leaf also shall not wither; and whatsoever he doeth shall prosper.

Finally, if you enjoyed this book, please take the time to share your thoughts and post a review on Amazon. It'd be greatly appreciated!

Many Thanks,

Brian Mahoney

We want to thank you for the purchase of this book and more importantly, thank you for reading it to the end. We hope your reading experience was pleasurable and that you would inform your family and friends on Facebook, Twitter or other social media.

We would like to continue to provide you with high-quality books, and that end, would you mind leaving us a review on Amazon.com?

Book Review link:

http://amazon.com/review/create-review/asin=B0B93G59J8

We are extremely grateful for your assistance.
Warm Regards, MahoneyProducts Publishing

Book Link:

Customer reviews

4.6 out of 5 stars   4.6 out of 5
6 global ratings

5 star   64%
4 star   36%-
3 star 0% (0%)   0%
2 star 0% (0%)   0%
1 star 0% (0%)

Review this product
Share your thoughts with other customers
(Write a Customer Review)

You might also enjoy:

Christian Book Series Self Help Bible Study Guide on Hell

KJV Bible Based Verses & Lessons for Men, Women, Couples, Teens, Kids, & Beginners

by Brian Mahoney

Christian Marriage Counseling Book of Bible Verses:

Marriage Scriptures to help Women, Men, Kids, Moms & Couples with Intimacy, Sex & Communication

Paperback – November 5, 2021

by Brian Mahoney (Author)

4.3   out of 5 stars 25 ratings

Marriage Book Amazon Link:

https://www.amazon.com/dp/B09L3NNZRR

Please leave a review

http://amazon.com/review/create-review/asin=B0B93G59J8

and then join Our VIP Mailing List Then Get Notified when we release our new books on FREE promotions.

FREE Amazon ebooks and free Audible ACX audio books!

Just click or Type in the Link Below

https://urlzs.com/HfbGF